WITHDRAWN

Illustrated
Histories of
**TWENTIETH
CENTURY
ARMS**

BRITISH AND AMERICAN
INFANTRY WEAPONS
OF WORLD WAR II

Other volumes in this series

GERMAN INFANTRY WEAPONS OF WORLD WAR II
by A. J. Barker

TANKS OF WORLD WAR I: BRITISH AND AMERICAN
by Peter Chamberlain and Chris Ellis

ALLIED BAYONETS OF WORLD WAR II
by J. Anthony Carter

1. (*top*) British soldiers in action with Vickers machine guns in Holland, 1944.

2. (*above*) United States soldiers in action with 60mm mortar on Pacific Island, 1945.

BRITISH AND AMERICAN INFANTRY WEAPONS OF WORLD WAR II

by

A. J. BARKER

ARCO PUBLISHING COMPANY, INC
New York

Published by ARCO PUBLISHING COMPANY, INC.,
219 Park Avenue South, New York, N.Y. 10003

Library of Congress Catalog Number 69–13594
Arco Book Number 668–01865–8

© A. J. Barker, 1969

Plates 2, 13, 23, 25, 27–30, 32, 34, 38–42, 45, 49, 54, 58 and 60 **are reproduced** by courtesy of the Imperial War Museum, London.

Printed in Great Britain

Contents

"Let us be clear about three facts. First, all battles and all wars are won in the end by infantrymen. Secondly, the infantryman always bears the brunt. His casualties are heavier, he suffers greater extremes of discomfort and fatigue than other arms. Thirdly, the art of the infantryman is less stereotyped and far harder to acquire in modern war than that of any other arm."

Field Marshal Viscount Wavell

BRITISH AND AMERICAN
INFANTRY WEAPONS OF WORLD WAR II

During the Second World War British standard pattern equipment was augmented with supplies of similar equipment manufactured in America. When the United States entered the war supplies of such equipment were increased under the Lend–Lease Agreement and, if Japan had not capitulated in 1945, it is probable that the proportion of weapons of United States origin in service with the British troops fighting in the Far East would have increased still further. Because of this and the fact that victory was an Allied achievement it is logical to review in the following pages the infantry weapons of the two nations together.

Differences in the organisation of the infantry units in the British and United States Armies are less important than the fact that a great variety of weapons had to be mastered by Allied and German infantrymen alike. For generations the infantryman had been regarded as inferior in technical ability and only useful with rifle and bayonet. Between 1939 and 1946 however, he was required to master a greater variety of weapons than any other branch of the Army. Contributory factors were the increasing need for anti-tank weapons and, for flushing Japanese bunkers, flamethrowers. But the idea of fire-power and tactics developed during the First World War had the greatest influence on the infantry weapons of 1939–1945. How the Germans went about solving the problem of the variety of small arms equipments is described in a companion volume to this, and it is interesting to compare German equipment with that of the Allies.

SMALL ARMS AMMUNITION

Britain

Three main types of small arms ammunition were used by the British infantry: ·303in, 9mm and the ·38in. A further type, the 7·92mm was used for tank machine guns. The ·303in round was used in rifles and machine guns, and by employing this round Britain became almost the last of the major powers to retain a rimmed cartridge. Such a cartridge has certain definite advantages when used with a hand operated bolt action rifle of the Lee Enfield type but with automatic weapons it complicates design and increases the number and types of weapon stoppages. Thus its retention at a time when the basis of fire power depended upon the use of automatic weapons was unsound. This policy however was dictated by the weapon stocks and production facilities in existence at the outbreak of war. (The war also revealed that British small arms ammunition was too powerful and heavy for normal engagements.)

9mm ammunition was introduced for use with sub-machine guns in the early stages of the war, and with adequate stopping power at the shorter ranges it proved itself an efficient round. The same ammunition was used extensively by the German Army and is used and manufactured today by many countries. It did what was expected of it and there were few complaints against either its characteristics or its performance. The few minor criticisms which came to light were nearly always attributable to faulty production.

·38 ammunition was used in pistols only. It is a rimmed cartridge of low muzzle velocity and its continued employment meant that it militated against the development of a self-loading pistol of the type used by other major powers. It also had an inferior all round performance to that of the 9mm round, and was an extra type of ammunition which unnecessarily elaborated both supply and production. In addition to these basic disadvantages minor defects arose as a result of production faults. A large number of rounds were manufactured with an excessive or inadequate charge weight. It was impossible to detect such rounds, and since weapons were often damaged in firing them, the large stocks suspected were condemned.

United States

As in Britain there was little development of small arms ammunition in the United States between the two wars. The ·300in standard American rifle cartridge was used for rifles and machine guns throughout the war; the ·45in round for pistols and sub-machine guns and ·300in American carbine cartridge for the light-weight semi-automatic carbine. Between 1940 and 1945 more than 47 billion rounds of S.A.A.—at a cost of about two and a half billion dollars—were manufactured in the U.S.

All this ammunition was rimless and there were few criticisms of its reliability. When fired from both pistols and sub-machine guns the ·45in calibre rounds were considered to have a relatively higher stopping power than the equivalent 9mm ammunition, and for this reason were favoured by the Americans.

RIFLES

Britain

Britain fought the war with ostensibly the same rifle as was used in 1914–1918. The No 4 Lee Enfield was a redesign of the No 1, adapted to cater for the techniques of mass production. Because it proved to be too heavy and cumbersome, especially in the Far East, a specially lightened version, the No 5 rifle was produced. For those confused by the nomenclature associated with the British "Marks" of rifle it is perhaps desirable to explain that there have been six marks of the Short Magazine Lee Enfield Rifle (SMLE).

Mk 1: approved 1902

Mk 2: similar to Mk 1 but a conversion from the earlier "Long" rifle

Mk 3: approved 1907

Mk 4: conversion from Mks 1 and 2 and similar to Mk 3.

Mk 3*: approved 1918. A simplified version of the Mk 3.

Mk 5: approved in 1922: an improvement on Mk 3.

Mk 6: an improvement on the Mk 5 and known now as the No 4

In 1941 the Mks 3 and 3* were renamed Rifle No 1, Mk 3 (or 3*) and the Mk 6 became the Rifle No 4

Other rifles in service with the British Forces included the ·303in Pattern '14 (P 14)—a conversion from a ·276in calibre design under consideration for re-arming the British Army in 1914, and manufactured in the United States—and the ·303in Canadian Ross Rifle. As soon as standard equipment became available, however, both the P 14 and the Ross were replaced in first-line battalions.

United States

When the United States entered the First World War her standard service rifle was the Springfield ·300in Model 1903. Having insufficient of these, she had to augment her supplies by increased production. Having been making the ·303in P 14 for Britain she turned to this design and converted it to suit the U.S. ·300 rimless cartridge. The resultant rifle was the Model '17 (frequently erroneously called in Britain the "Springfield" and in the U.S. often called the "American Enfield".)

These two rifles were the standard hand-operated bolt action rifles of the U.S. Forces at the beginning of the Second World War. But unlike Britain, the United States had developed and was taking into service a self-loading rifle—the Garand. In 1939 mass production of this rifle started and was issued to the troops as it became available. Thus it was that General McArthur's troops, who had been re-equipped with the Garand shortly before the Japanese attack, gave the weapon its battle initiation. And on 20 February 1942 McArthur cabled General Marshall to say that "Garand rifles [are] giving superior service to Springfield . . . these weapons are excellent . . ." Additionally, the ·300in self-loading carbine—the "M1"— had also been evolved as a substitute for the pistol. Carried by officers, NCOs and others previously armed with the Colt Automatic pistol, it was an attempt to combine the advantages of a light rifle with those of a weapon for personal defence.

PISTOLS AND REVOLVERS

Britain

Most of the British Forces during the war were equipped with a revolver-type pistol firing ·38 calibre ammunition, but even up to 1942 quite a number of old ·455in Webley and Colt revolvers were in service. Self-loading pistols of American design were used by airborne and other specialist troops. (They were so popular that by 1945 it had become obvious that a self-loading pistol firing the same 9mm ammunition as the sub-machine gun was needed in the British Army.)

United States

Like most countries, the United States had discarded the revolver in favour of a self-loading pistol long before the outbreak of war. Not only does the self-loading pistol have a greater magazine capacity and it can be loaded more quickly, the soldier can be taught to shoot it in less time. Thus, although the ·45in Smith and Wesson 1917 revolver was still in service, the standard equipment became the ·45in 1911 and 1911A1 Automatic—a Colt design of proven worth.

SUB-MACHINE GUNS

Britain

Between the wars the British Army had ignored the possibilities of the sub-machine gun—the gangsters' weapon—which was light, handy and of considerable firepower. But experience soon showed that it was a deadly weapon in street and close quarter fighting at ranges up to 75 yards. In the first year of the war Britain bought limited quantities of the original M.1928 Thompson—an expensive, precision-made weapon. Later the "Sten Machine Carbine" was developed and introduced as the standard close range assault weapon. It was cheap and easy to produce, but it had many serious faults and was never popular. Not only did it prove to be unreliable and later models heavy and cumbersome, but the standard of production was often poor and this aggravated the defects inherent in the design.

United States

During America's era of Prohibition the Thompson sub-machine gun had been extensively used by law-breaking gangs, and its value as a weapon to the Army had been appreciated—though perhaps not to the extent visualised later. The U.S. Army took the M.1928 model into limited service in the early part of the war but this was partially displaced by the M.1—a cheapened version of the M.1928 —until both models were superseded by the cheap mass-produced ·45in M.3 gun which equated to the British Sten and German Schmeisser MP.38.

MACHINE GUNS

Britain

The Bren light machine gun bore the brunt of the British infantry small arms fighting. It was an outstanding success, and there can be little doubt that it was one of the best contemporary light machine guns in use by any army. Most of the war-time criticisms of the weapon were attributable to its use of rimmed ammunition. But its main disadvantage was its weight and although attempts were made to lighten it no appreciable reduction in its weight was found to be possible.

In India some infantry battalions were equipped with the Vickers–Berthier light machine gun, and a few of these weapons were issued to second line units in the United Kingdom in 1940. A number of old Lewis light machine guns—British ·303in, and U.S. ·300in weapons originally designed for use in aircraft and modified in

Britain for ground use—were also issued as infantry weapons to the Local Defence Volunteers (later to be known as the Home Guard). But such weapons were not standard fighting equipment and it was the Bren that remained the conventional British infantry section weapon throughout the war.

As a "medium" machine gun the old Vickers, which had been used extensively in the First World War, proved its value. Despite its age, fighting under all conditions proved it to be a reliable weapon with an excellent performance of sustained and effective fire. Its main disadvantages were its excessive weight and its reliance on water for cooling purposes. It also has a complicated mechanism and a diversity of weapon stoppages, both of which factors add to the time taken for training and tend to decrease the operational value of the gun. At times the operational need for a medium machine gun as well as the Bren was questioned but experience showed that there was a requirement for a sustained fire machine gun of the Vickers type, and these sustained fire capabilities were exploited to the full.

United States

At a time when other powers hesitated because of the expense involved, the United States took the bold decision to re-equip their infantry with self-loading rifles. This now gave the American Infantry a sufficiency of firepower, and because of this the light machine gun no longer enjoyed the importance in the U.S. Army that it did in other armies which had retained the manual bolt-action rifles. At the same time the equivalent of the British Vickers "medium" machine gun—the Browning ·300 1917 or 1917A1— tended on occasions to be used tactically like the British Bren.

The U.S. ·300 Browning 1918 or 1918A1—the Browning Automatic Rifle—is in British parlance a light machine gun. A robust and reliable gun it served the U.S. infantry well. The "Johnson Light Machine Gun 1941" was a lighter weapon issued and used primarily by the U.S. Marines, Rangers and Special Forces. Towards the end of the war this gun was superseded by a slightly heavier but improved model, the Johnson 1944.

Little need be said about the standard U.S. medium machine gun, since the Browning, like the Vickers, is well known and has enjoyed an international reputation for reliability. Before the war it was manufactured and sold by Fabrique Nationale de Guerre at Herstal in Belgium, and both the Chinese and the Japanese imitated and manufactured the Browning. Like the British with the Vickers, the Americans found that the Browning could be relied upon to develop heavy sustained fire for very long periods, but they were heavy weapons and towards the end of the war they were regarded as obsolescent for long range fire.

MORTARS

Britain

The light 2in mortar, developed in the thirties, was soon recognised as a valuable and effective infantry weapon. Light and quick into action, it could concentrate fire on a given target with speed and accuracy. High explosive and smoke bombs both gave a good performance. But there were some ammunition defects and the mortar was also criticised for its limited maximum range of 500 yards. This limitation could be embarrassing when an illuminating bomb was fired in a strong adverse wind as it often floated back to light up the firer.

The standard "medium" mortar used throughout the war by British infantry battalions was the 3in, which had been developed from the Stokes trench mortar of the First World War. As a lethal weapon it had few equals on the battlefield, but its bombs were manufactured in cast iron—a policy made necessary by the type of productive capacity available in war-time Britain. Cast iron bombs are extremely effective but they could not be manufactured to the same close tolerances as machine finished bombs. Thus accuracy suffered. Nevertheless, the 3-inch mortar remained in the British service throughout the war—and long afterwards.

See also Appendix 6.

United States

The United States war-time light mortar was the 60mm M2. Of French origin, developed by the Brandt Company, it was manufactured in the United States to designs altered to conform with U.S. standards. Unlike the British 2in mortar which was primarily a platoon weapon, the 60mm mortar was essentially a company support weapon firing a relatively heavy bomb (3 lb) to a range of 2,000 yards, and employing a crew of five men. (The British 2in weapon fired a 2lb bomb 500 yards and was operated by a two-man crew.)

Throughout the war, the U.S. medium mortar was the 81mm M1. During the First World War, the standard mortar for indirect fire used by the U.S. infantry was the British 3in Stokes trench mortar Mk 1. Designs for a new mortar were started in 1920, but these were abandoned in favour of attempts to attain greater accuracy with the ammunition. While this development work was progressing, the

Brandt firm succeeded in developing a refined version of the Stokes mortar, together with suitable ammunition and this was adopted by the U.S. War Department.

Towards the end of the war an improved 81mm mortar, termed the "Universal" was developed. This weapon was lighter and had a shorter tube.

ANTI-TANK WEAPONS

Britain

In 1939, the British infantry went to war with only one anti-tank weapon: the Boys anti-tank rifle—a high velocity ground mounted rifle firing a ·55in calibre bullet. It was a relatively heavy weapon and, despite the attachment of a recoil reducer, always induced considerable gun shyness among its users. For this reason it was never popular, and since its performance was inadequate even at the time of its introduction and it was possible to effect only limited improvements to the ammunition, it soon became outmoded and due for replacement.

The P.I.A.T. was the replacement weapon. This utilised a hollow charge projectile and was effective in the anti-tank role to a range of about 75 yards. Its penetration of 100mm was a considerable improvement on the Boys rifle but it suffered the defects of excessive weight (32lbs) and the fact that owing to its short range it was not always possible to site it to engage flank targets. Thus it was often outclassed by the heavy frontal armour presented as a target. As it was as a short range weapon, a certainty of first round hit and "kill" was most desirable from the firer's point of view, since his position was usually disclosed by the act of firing. P.I.A.T. ammunition suffered from serious defects under conditions of prolonged storage, the most grave being the deterioration of the azide fuze. The danger from premature detonation was so great that after the war all training with the P.I.A.T. was prohibited.

The only offensive anti-tank weapon of greater than throwing range which was generally available to the British infantry was the No 68 grenade. This was projected from a cup discharger fixed to the No 1 rifle. It employed the hollow charge principle but its armour penetration was never adequate against any but the more lightly armoured vehicles. Since its range was short, this was primarily a "last-ditch" weapon and more often than not the target presented was the front and most thickly-armoured portion of the tank. Consequently the grenade was soon outmatched by improvements in armour and never played a significant part in anti-tank engagements.

14

To kill tanks the infantry placed most reliance on the high velocity guns with which each first line battalion was issued. Unfortunately the development of such guns always tended to lag behind that of the German tanks, and guns were therefore outmoded either before or soon after their introduction to service by more thickly armoured targets. Nevertheless, there was a considerable improvement of infantry anti-tank armaments as the war progressed. At the beginning the French 25mm Hotchkiss equipment was standard. This was later replaced by the 2 pounder which in turn gave way to the 6 pounder. Even this gun, large and cumbersome though it was, proved incapable of defeating the heavier German tanks and at the end of the war the 17 pounder was introduced as the standard infantry anti-tank equipment. At this stage it was obvious that a new principle of anti-tank attack was required. The 17-pounder gun weighed over 3 tons and it was most difficult to tow and to handle into infantry positions. Its flash on firing was easily seen and it was difficult to conceal.

United States

Experience gained by the British Army in the period preceding the entry of the United States into the war was not lost on the Americans. Furthermore, they had already realised that killing tanks was a far greater problem than had been appreciated in Europe. The Germans and Russians had been using rocket firing weapons for some years. It was the Americans, however, who adopted the rocket projector as a means of launching an efficient anti-tank projectile, and the U.S. 2·36in "Bazooka" was the first weapon of its kind. Subsequently the Germans captured Bazookas from the Russians—to whom they were lease-lent—and copied them.

One of the great arms achievements of the U.S. Ordnance Department was the development of the first really portable artillery which could be carried by the infantry. The principle of recoilless weapons was not new—indeed it had been used by the Germans on aircraft cannon in the First World War—and it reappeared on German airborne artillery during 1942. By 1944 Britain also had recoilless guns, but early in 1945 the Americans were the first of the Allies to use such weapons and thereafter the 57mm and 75mm equipment became standard with their airborne forces. In the Pacific campaign these weapons proved their worth in many ways. Not only were they used against Japanese bunkers and fortified caves, where accuracy and striking power were of prime importance, but they were also used for conventional artillery work in regions where the conventional artillery could not operate.

BAYONETS

Bayonets and commando knives were, and are, an essential part of an infantryman's equipment—although from the information available it appears that the number of casualties resulting from their use in the Second World War was comparatively small. This is understandable; in the final stages of an assault the *threat* of cold steel is usually enough. A variety of British bayonets were produced as the war progressed and an illustration of those which became service issues will be found on page 26.

The United States was less concerned with the development of bayonets than with other weapons. A specialised study of bayonets is published in a companion volume in this series.

GRENADES

Both the British and United States infantry used anti-personnel hand grenades of a comparable type in the war. Such grenades were slightly heavy but possessed considerable lethal power, although throwing them was made difficult by the complicated operation of their arming devices. Special mention must be made of the British 69 grenade—a light plastic grenade of great bursting effect which was neither effective nor popular. These grenades, developed early in the war, were often the source of fatal accidents, and their danger to Allied troops was so disproportionate to its effects on the enemy that it was taken out of service in 1943.

Anti-tank grenades were never popular in the United States army, and none of those used by the British infantry were of significant value since they all suffered from the same limitations of short range, excessive weight and poor destructive capacity. Of the British grenades, the 75 or Hawkins grenade mine, which was used extensively as a track cutting mine, for booby traps and general purposes, was the most efficient. The 82 (Gammon Bomb) was used by airborne troops more for demolition purposes than in its anti-tank role; the 73 or Thermos Grenade was found to have too little power, and its successor the 74 or "Sticky" Grenade was dangerous to use because it often affixed itself firmly to the thrower as he swung his arm, and results were usually fatal.

A variety of smoke grenades was also employed by both armies for both obscuration and signalling.

FLAME THROWERS

Flame throwers were not employed by the British infantry until 1943. Two types were used and as both were developed rapidly,

16

many defects became apparent after a short period in service. Nevertheless, they proved to be particularly effective against troops who were so protected as to be immune to other weapons, i.e. against bunkers and buildings. They also had a considerable psychological effect upon other troops in the immediate vicinity.

The Man-borne Flame Thrower

The "life-buoy" flame thrower was used in Burma and North West Europe from 1944 until the end of the war. It was heavy, weighing 65lb and had a normal range of well under 40 yards. Furthermore, its ignition system of a spark-lit hydrogen jet was uncertain. Its heavy weight, short range and uncertainty of action, coupled with the vulnerability of the operator and difficulties in the supply of fuel and hydrogen made the equipment unpopular under conditions which were ideal for its use. The "life-buoy" was replaced in 1945 by the Ack-Pack flame-thrower which is still in use in the British Army. This equipment was lighter (48lb), used a ten shot cartridge igniter system and has a range of nearly 50 yards.

The Carrier-borne Flame Thrower

The Wasp equipment, mounted in the British infantry's universal carrier, was used in the latter stages of the war. It had a fuel capacity of 79 gallons and a range of about 120 yards. Owing to this shortness of range and to the vulnerability of the carrier and its crew, the number of occasions on which it could be employed were limited.

17

SMALL ARMS AMMUNITION

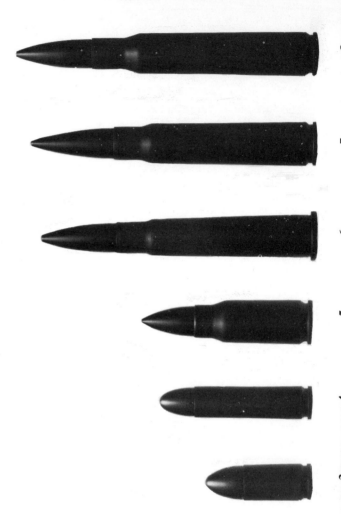

British and U.S. Infantry Ammunition of 1939–1945 compared with its German equivalents

Plate number		3	4	5	6	7	8
Type		9mm	American ·300in short	German short 7·92mm	British ·303in	Mauser 7·92mm	American ·300in
Used in		Machine carbine	Machine carbine	Machine carbine	M.G. L.M.G. Rifle	M.G. L.M.G. Rifle	M.G. Rifle
Muzzle energy	Kgm ft lb	50 362	120 868	200 1,440	335 2,430	370 2,680	360 2,530
Weight of one Round	grams grains	12 185	12·65 195	16·6 256	24·9 384	26·5 409	25·7 390
Weight of 100 Rounds	kg lb	1·200 2·64	1·270 2·8	1·650 3·63	2·500 5·50	2·650 5·84	2·550 5·65
Length of Round	mm in	29·5 1·16	42·7 1·675	27·8 1·88	77·3 3·04	80·4 3·16	84·6 3·34

9. *No 1 Mk 3*

This rifle stayed with the British Army throughout the war, although issues of the new No 4 rifle produced in Britain, Canada and the U.S.A. started in late 1942, and by the end of the North African campaign only about 50% of the troops in the Middle East were still armed with the No. 1. Pre-war manufactured, when a high standard of workmanship could be maintained, there were few complaints about the "No 1".

No 2 Mk 4

A training rifle, the No 2 Mk 4 was identical with the No 1 except that it had a ·22 barrel and modified bolt head for rim fire cartridges.

10, 11. *No 3 Mk 1* and *Mk 1**

"No 3" was the official designation of the "P 14", manufactured
in the United States. Because the
P 14 is extremely accurate at short
ranges it was sometimes used—in
the absence of any better equipment
in 1940—by snipers.

12. *No 4 Mk 1*

This was a wartime mass produced rifle of the British infantry. The well tried design of its predecessors was sound, but when it was first issued there were many complaints about its performance. Most of the faults were traced back to mass production under adverse conditions.

13. *No 5 Mk 1*

Developed originally for use in the Far East the No 5 Rifle was a modified version of the No 4. The wooden furniture was reduced to a minimum and the barrel cut down. To compensate for increased kick and flash, a rubber butt pad and flash eliminator were fitted.

Sniping Equipment in the British Army

Even after the outbreak of war no steps were taken to provide sniping rifles for the Army then building up until, in December 1939, it was decided to try to make do with the No 4 rifle—not then in production—and the No 32 telescopic sight—designed for the Bren and also not yet in production. These two were to be joined together with a bracket which was not even on the drawing board at that stage. During 1940 there was little call for sniping rifles from the forces in the field. However, in the Spring of 1941 the first of the new sniping rifles were beginning to come off the production line when it was decided to close down the Sniping Wing of the Small Arms School at Bisley to make way for an anti-aircraft training establishment. There was, therefore, no competent 'user' body available or qualified to try out and comment upon this new equipment. This fact was to have unfortunate results later on.

14. *The ·303in Pattern '14 (P 14)*

Service designation: Rifle No 3 Mk 1*

Basic data:

Weight: 9lb 6oz
Length: 3ft 10½in
Magazine capacity: 5 rounds

British S.M.L.E. Rifles: Comparative Data

Service Designation	No 1	No 2	No 3	No 4	No 5
Weight	8lb 10½oz	8lb 12½oz	9lb 6oz	8lb 15oz	7lb 2½oz
Length	3ft 8½in	3ft 8½in	3ft 10½in	3ft 8½in	3ft 3½in
Rifling	5 grooves left hand twist 1 in 10				
Sighting Radius	19·44in	19·44in	31·75in	28·72in	23in

Magazine capacity for the No 1, No 4 and No 5 service rifles was 10 rounds, and that for the No 3 five rounds.

15. *Bayonets*

This shows the development of
British bayonets from 1935 to 1945.
At the outbreak of the war the
infantry were equipped with the
old "long" Lee–Enfield bayonet of
the First World War (*bottom
bayonets*). Because the authorities
considered it to be too long and
clumsy attempts were made to
introduce a replacement "spike",
designed between the wars (*central
bayonets*). In the Middle East it was
especially unpopular with the Aus-
tralians who complained that it
made them the laughing stock of the
Italians. Subsequently it was decided
that what was needed was a bayonet
which could serve as a patrol knife
as well as a lethal projection fitted
to the muzzle of a rifle (*top bayonets*).

16. *·300in Springfield Rifle M 1903*

Basic data:

Calibre: ·300
Feed: Magazine, 5 rounds
Muzzle velocity: 2,700f/s
Bullet weight: 150 grains
Length overall: 3ft 7¼in
Length barrel: 24in
Weight: 8·69lb
Sights: Front blade, rear leaf
    U 100–2,350 yards
Range: Effective 600 yards

17. *U.S. Rifle ·300in M 1 (Garand)*

Basic data:

Calibre: ·300in
Feed: Magazine clip 8 rounds
Muzzle velocity: 2,700f/s
Bullet weight: 150 grains
Length overall: 3ft 7in
Length barrel: 24in
Weight: 9½lb
Sights: Aperture adjustable
 100–1,200 yards
Method of operation: Gas
Type of fire: Single shots

With a telescopic sight this weapon was also used as a sniper's rifle.

According to General George Patton in January 1945 the Garand was "the greatest battle implement ever designed". At that time the U.S. Army was the only one in the world fully equipped with self-loading rifles.

Early in 1943, a grenade launcher (M 7) was brought into service for use with this rifle. A soldier equipped with one of these grenade launchers could fire anti-tank and anti-personnel grenades as well as signal flares to a range of 300 yards.

18. *·300in "Enfield" 1917 Rifle*

Except that this rifle has a ·300in calibre, the physical details (below) are approximately the same as for the British No 3 Mk 1 (P 14).

Basic data:

Calibre: ·300in
Feed: Magazine, 5 rounds
Muzzle velocity: 2,700f/s
Bullet weight: 150 grains
Length overall: 46·3in
Length barrel: 26in
Weight: 9lb 6oz
Sights: Blade front, leaf back-sight aperture 200–900 yards

19. ·300*in M 1 Carbine*

Mass production of the M 1 carbine, weighing five and a half pounds, with a 15-round magazine, started in 1941 and a total of 5·5 million were manufactured for service in the war. A modification of the same calibre, equipped with a folding stock for use by airborne troops and called M 1A1 was adopted in May 1942 and a large number of these was also produced. As the war progressed the infantry clamoured for increased firepower and the original self-loading M 1 was modified to make it capable of firing selective semi- and fully-automatic fire. This modified carbine, designated the M 2, was given a 30 round magazine and adopted in October 1944. More than 550,000 were produced for issue to front-line troops.

Basic data (original M 1 carbine):

Calibre: ·300in
Feed: Magazine, 15 rounds
Muzzle velocity: 2,000f/s
Bullet weight: 110 grains
Length overall: 35½in
Length barrel: 18in
Weight: 5½lb
Sights: Blade front, aperture 100 to 300 yards
Range: Accurate 300 yards
Range maximum: About 2,000 yards
Method of operation: Gas
Type of fire: Single shot only
(*Note:* M1A1 Folding stock M2 Automatic)

U.S. Sniper's Rifle M1903A4

Until the Garand became available to permit a general replacement of the Springfield rifle the ·300 Springfield remained in service. However, the latter was used throughout the war as a sniping rifle—being equipped with a telescopic sight for this purpose.

Basic data:

Weight with "Weaver" telescopic sight: 9lb 2oz
Weight with Lyman Alaskan sight: 9lb 6oz
Sight magnification: 2½ ×
Eye relief: 3 to 5in
(Other characteristics as for the Springfield ·300in M1903A1)

PISTOLS AND REVOLVERS

Britain

A variety of pistols saw service in the British Army during the war. Basic data for the five main types are given.

20. *Pistol No 2 Mk 1 Revolver*

Basic data:

Calibre: ·380in RH 7 grooves
Cylinder: 6 rounds
Muzzle velocity: 600 f/s
Bullet weight: 200 grains
Length overall: 10½in
Length barrel: 5in
Weight: 27·5oz
Range: Max. 1,100 yards at 30°

21. *Smith and Wesson No 2 Revolver*

Basic data:

Calibre: ·380in
Cylinder: 6 rounds
Muzzle velocity: 600f/s
Bullet weight: 200 grains
Length overall: $10\frac{1}{8}$in
Length barrel: 5in
Weight: 31oz
Sights: Front fixed
    Rear, square notch

33

22. *Webley · 455in No 1 Mk VI Revolver*

Basic data:

Calibre: ·455, RH 7 grooves
Cylinder: 6 rounds
Muzzle velocity: About 600f/s
Bullet weight: 255 grains
Length overall: 11¼in
Length barrel: 6in
Weight: 38oz
Sights: Fixed
Range: Accurate 50 yards
Range maximum: 800 yards
Type of action: Hinged frame.
　　　Double action

23. *Webley S.L. Pistol*

Basic data:

Calibre:	·455in
Feed:	Magazine
Capacity:	7 rounds
Muzzle velocity:	750f/s
Bullet weight:	220 grains
Length overall:	8½in
Length barrel:	5in
Weight:	39oz
Sights:	Fixed
Range:	Accurate 75 yards
Range maximum:	1,500 yards
Method of operation:	Recoil
Type of fire:	Single shot only

British Colt S.L. Pistol

Basic data:

Calibre:	·455in
Feed:	Magazine
Capacity:	7 rounds
Muzzle velocity:	750f/s
Bullet weight:	220 grains
Length overall:	8½in
Length barrel:	5in
Weight:	39oz
Sights:	Fixed
Range:	Accurate 75 yards
Range maximum:	1,500 yards
Method of operation:	Recoil

24. *Colt 1911 S.L. Pistol*

The ·45in Colt "automatic" was adopted by the United States Army in 1911 and used throughout the First World War. During the Second War it continued as the standard personal weapon, but as its importance declined, those who were armed with a pistol were re-equipped with a carbine or sub-machine gun.

Basic data:

Calibre: ·45in
Feed: Magazine
Capacity: 7 rounds
Muzzle velocity: 810f/s
Bullet weight: 230 grains
Length overall: 8½in
Length barrel: 5in
Weight: 39oz
Sight: Partridge type, fixed
Range: Accurate 75 yards
Range maximum: 1,600 yards
Method of operation: Recoil
Type of fire: Single shot

SUB-MACHINE GUNS—*Britain*

In the first two years of the war, before the Sten gun was designed, a limited number of Thompson sub-machine guns were purchased in the United States and issued on a limited scale to some British infantry units.

25. *1928 Model*

Basic data:
    Calibre: ·45in
    Feed: Magazine, 20 rounds, drum 50 and 100 rounds
    Muzzle velocity: 920f/s
    Length overall: 33in
    Length barrel: 10½in
    Weight: 9lb 13oz
    Sight: Front blade, rear aperture, graduated to 600 yards
    Range: Accurate, about 300 yards
    Method of operation: Case projection
    Cooling: Air
    Type of fire: Single and automatic
    Cyclic rate of fire: 600 to 700rpm

26.-31. *Sten Gun*

The 9mm Sten ran through a number of "Marks"—close on a million weapons being manufactured during its service, and large numbers were supplied to resistance units in occupied territory.

Basic data:

Calibre: 9mm, 6 grooves, RH
Feed: Magazine, 32 rounds
Muzzle velocity: 1,425f/s
Bullet weight: 125 grains
Length overall: 30in (Mk 5) (Mk 2 32in)
Length barrel: 7⅜in
Weight: 6½ to 8lb according to the *Mk*
Sights: Adjustable blade, fore. Fixed back for 100 yards
Range: Approx. max. range about 200 yards
Method of operation: Case projection
Type of fire: Single and automatic
Cyclic rate of fire: 500 to 550 per minute
Cooled: Air

26. *Mark 2*

38

Sten guns

27. *Mark 1*   **28.** *Mark 2*   **29.** *Mark 3*   **30.** *Mark 4*

With Marks 1 and 2, care had to be taken that the left hand gripped the barrel well forward, so that none of the fingers entered the ejection opening or they would be trapped by the breech-block—a painful proceeding. In the Mark 3 a small flange in front of the ejection opening prevented this. Unlike the Thompson, it was not necessary to oil the Sten and it continued to fire in a bone dry condition.

31. *Mark 5*

SUB-MACHINE GUNS—*United States*

The Thompson M 1928A1 was in service at the beginning of the war. (Details will be found in the preceding section.) In the course of the war the weapon was modified and a new Thompson M1A1 was issued. But both weapons were superseded in 1943 by the SMG M3.

The Thompson was a good gun, but it was expensive and difficult to manufacture. The replacement weapon, the M 3, was not only considerably cheaper ($18 as compared with $55 for the Thompson) but it had greater accuracy and reliability.

32. ·*45in M 3 Sub-machine gun*

Basic data:

Calibre: ·45in
Feed: Magazine, 30 rounds
Muzzle velocity: 920f/s
Length overall: Stock extended 29·8in. Stock closed 22·8in
Length barrel: 8in
Weight: 8lb 1oz
Sights: Fixed, aperture rear
Range: Standard, about 300 yards
Method of operation: Case projection
Cooling: Air
Type of fire: Automatic only
Rate of fire: 450rpm

33

MACHINE GUNS—*Britain*

Between the wars it was decided that the British Army needed a light machine gun to replace the old Lewis gun. This had given good service in the First World War but was cumbersome and often prone to stoppages. Numerous trials and experiments were staged to determine the best gun available and in 1925 a prize of £3,000 was offered for the best weapon in a series of trials. Of the many entries, including weapons of Madsen (Denmark), Hotchkiss and Browning, the Czech "ZB" came out best and Britain chose to adopt a modified version which was called the "Bren". The name was derived from the first two letters of Brno, its place of origin in Czechoslovakia, and the first two letters of Enfield, where it was manufactured.

The Vickers Berthier light machine gun ("VB") which has a similar appearance to the Bren, did well in the same competition and because the Indian Army wanted a new LMG urgently, India chose to adopt the VB.

Each gun had a spare barrel and after ten magazines had been fired at the rapid rate (3 magazines a minute) it was recommended that the barrels should be changed.

Originally each gun had its own tripod on which it could be used against ground or airborne targets. But by 1943 it had been decided that

41

34

one tripod for every three guns was all that was necessary since the occasions on which the gun was used as a medium machine gun were extremely rare. As an anti-aircraft mounting the tripod left much to be desired and this role was also abandoned when it was found that the practice of shooting at fast-moving aircraft was of extremely doubtful value—and, more often than not, merely wasted ammunition.

33, 34. *·303in Bren Mk 1*

Basic data:

> Calibre: ·303in, 6 grooves, RH
> Feed: Box magazine, 30 and 100 rounds
> Muzzle velocity: 2,440f/s
> Bullet weight: 174 grains
> Length: $45\frac{3}{8}$in
> Weight: 22lb
> Sights: Fixed fore. Aperture rear. 200–2,000 yards
> Range: Accurate 500 yards
> Method of operation: Gas
> Type of fire: Single or automatic
> Cyclic rate of fire: 450–550rpm
> Cooling: Air

·303in "VB"

Basic data:

Weight: 24lb
Length overall: 45½in
Feed: Vertical box magazine, Bren type
Capacity of magazine: 30 rounds
Weight of magazine: Empty 12oz. Full 2lb 7oz
System of operation: Gas operated
Feed opening: Top
Ejection: Right side
Cocking handle: Right side
Calibre: ·303in
Ammunition: ·303in British service
Type of fire: Single shot or automatic
Rate of fire: 500–600rpm

The Mark 1 gun was the first VB issued to troops of the Indian Army. Improvements in the later models, culminating in the Mk 3 included a simple recoil reducer (muzzle brake) and a simplified trigger mechanism as well as the incorporation of recoiling movement of the body in the receiver—as in the Bren.

·303in Vickers Medium Machine Gun

The Vickers MMG embodies the oldest type action—that of the Maxim.

The Mk 1 weapon
Basic data:

Calibre: ·303in, 5 grooves, LH
Feed: Fabric belt, 250 rounds
Muzzle velocity: 2,440f/s
Bullet weight: 174 grains
Length overall: 3ft 8in
Length barrel: $24\frac{1}{4}$in ($28\frac{3}{4}$in on earlier model)
Weight: $32\frac{1}{2}$lb without water
       $42\frac{1}{2}$lb with water
Sights: Foresight blades, Backsight Tangent aperture
Range: 2,000 yards (Mk VII ammunition)
     4,000 yards (Mk VIII streamlined ammunition)
Method of operation: Recoil
Type of fire: Automatic only
Cyclic rate of fire: 500rpm
Cooling: Water.

35. *Mk 1 on mounting tripod Mk 4B*

44

36 (top). *Vickers machine gun on the outskirts of Audrieu, Normandy*

37 (above). *Vickers machine gun in action, near Nijmegen, Holland*

45

MACHINE GUNS—*United States*

38. *Browning Automatic Rifle*

The BAR was one of the weapons designed by Mr. Browning and accepted in the U.S. Army in 1917.

Basic data:

Weight with tripod: 19·4lb
Weight of barrel: 3·65lb
Length of barrel: 24·1in
Length overall: 47·8in
Rifling: 4 grooves; Right-hand twist 1 turn in 10in
Operation: Gas
Cooling: Air
Rate of fire: 500rpm
Feed: Magazine 20 rounds
Muzzle velocity: 2,680 f/s
Sights: Blade front, aperture rear, graduated to 1,600 yards
Range: Accurate 600 yards

46

39. *Browning ·300in M1917A1 (Medium) Machine Gun*

The Browning M1917A1 machine gun was the American Army's equivalent of the British Vickers. With its water-cooled barrel it was able to sustain fire for longer than would have been possible with similar air-cooled weapons of the time.

Basic data:

Calibre: ·300in
Feed: Fabric belt, 250 rounds
Muzzle velocity: 2,800f/s
Bullet weight: 150 grains
Length overall: 38in
Length barrel: 24in
Weight: 33½lb
Sights: Blade front, tangent rear, zero to 2,600 yards, 2,800 metres or 3,400 yards
Range effective: 2,500 yards
Range maximum: 4,000 yards
Method of operation: Recoil
Cooling: Water ·
Cyclic rate of fire: 400–520rpm
Type of fire: Automatic only

There are ·50 weapons of this type. But they were not standard infantry weapons.

Browning ·50in M2 Machine Gun

This heavy calibre air-cooled machine gun was produced with three different types of barrel for use as an aircraft gun, as an anti-aircraft weapon (see note on the ·300 M.1917A1 Machine Gun) and as infantry equipment or tank gun. In this form it was known as the Model HB M2, Ground.

Basic data:

Calibre: ·50in
Feed: Fabric belt, 100 rounds
Muzzle velocity: 2,400f/s
Bullet weight: 705 grains
Length overall: 56in
Length barrel: 36in or 45in
Weight: 79lb with the 36in barrel
        84lb with the 45in barrel
Sights: Blade front; tangent rear
Range: Maximum 7,200 yards
Method of operation: Recoil
Cooling: Air
Cyclic rate of fire: 400–500rpm
Type of fire: Automatic only

MORTARS—*Britain*

The 2in mortar developed for the British Army in the thirties and similar to the Spanish 2in Ecia trench mortar, was similar to other light mortars developed by the other major European Powers, when it was decided that the rifle projected grenade gave insufficient close support to infantry.

40, 41. *Muzzle Loading Mortar Ordnance M.L. 2in*

Basic data:

(i) *Mortar*

Weight, with spade: 10½lb
Weight, with base: 19lb (approx) (Infantry model)
Maximum range: 500 yards
Minimum range: 100 yards
Maximum rate of fire: 8rpm
Elevation: May be fired high angle or low angle
Method of firing: Firing lever

(ii) *Ammunition*

Bombs

H.E.: 2lb 4oz (approx)
Smoke: 2lb (approx)
Illuminating: 1lb 1oz (approx)
Signal: 1–2lb (approx)

48

40

41

Propellant
Ballistite: 47 or 55 grains

Fuses
Percussion: 151, 151A or 161

Numerous modifications were made to this weapon after its intro-duction into the service in 1938. The various marks of equipments are as follows:

    (i) Used with Universal Carriers: Mks II*, II**, II***, VII, VII**, VIII*

    (ii) Used with Airborne Troops: Mks VII*, VIII

42, 43. *Medium 3in Mortar*

This smooth-bore, muzzle loading weapon was the direct descendant of the Stokes trench mortar of the First World War.

Basic data:

System of loading: Rounds are loaded singly from the muzzle end of barrel
Weights: Mortar: 44lb
        Base Plate: 37lb
        Mounting (including cradle): 45lb (approx)
Dimensions: Mortar: overall length: 28in
           Mounting: sight removed and cradle swung over-length: 36in
           Width, legs spread: 28in
           Width, legs folded: 10·5in
           Base plate: length 22·5in
                     width 14·25in
                     depth 9in
Maximum range: 2,800 yards — Originally this was 1,600 yards
Minimum range: 125 yards — Originally this was   275 yards
Elevation: 45° to 80°
Traverse: $5\frac{1}{2}°$—R and L of centre line
Transport: Universal Carrier or man-loads
Ammunition: 10lb, high explosive, smoke, and illuminating bombs could be fired from this weapon.

43

MORTARS—*United States*

M2 60mm Mortar

This mortar was not unlike the British 2in weapon in appearance. But because of its greater range and heavier bomb it could be considered to be in a different category tactically.

Basic data:

(i) *Mortar*

Weight of mortar, M2, and Mount, M2: 42·0lb
Weight of mortar: 12·8lb
Overall length of mortar: 28·6in
Diameter of bore: 2·36in
Rate of fire, maximum: 30 to 35rpm
Rate of fire, normal: 18rpm

(ii) *M2 Mounting*

Weight of mount: 29·2lb
Weight of bipod: 16·4lb
Weight of base place: 12·8lb
Elevations, approximate: 40° to 85°
Mortar clamp position A: 40° to 65°
Mortar clamp position B: 45° to 70°
Mortar clamp position C: 50° to 85°
Maximum traverse, right: 70mils
Maximum traverse, left: 70mils

(iii) *Ammunition*

Shell range: H.E. M49A2 ⎫
          Illuminating, M83 ⎬ 200 to 1,985 yards
          Training, M69 ⎭

44.

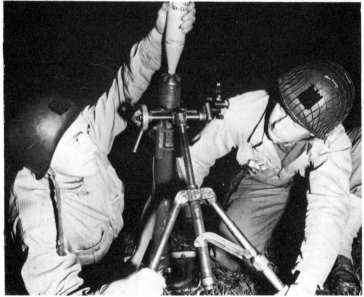

45.

53

46. *U.S. 81mm* (*Medium*) *Mortar M1*

Basic data:

(i) *Mortar*

Weight of mortar, M1, and Mount, M1: 136·0lb
Weight of mortar: 44·5lb
Overall length of mortar: 49·5in
Diameter bore: 3·2in
Rate of fire, maximum: 30 to 35rpm
Rate of fire, normal: 18rpm

(ii) *M1 Mounting*

Weight of mount: 91·5lb
Weight of bipod: 46·5lb
Weight of base plate: 45·0lb
Elevations, approximate: 40° to 85°
Mortar clamp position A: 40° to 70°
Mortar clamp position B: 50° to 80°
Mortar clamp position C: 55° to 85°
Maximum traverse, right: 90mils
Maximum traverse, left: 90mils

(iii) *Ammunition*

Weight: Ranges (approximate)
H.E. shell, M43A1, 6·87lb: 100 to 3,290 yards
M36. 10·62lb: 300 to 2,558 yards
Chemical shell, M57, 10·75lb: 300 to 2,470 yards

47. ·55in Boys Anti-Tank Rifle

ANTI-TANK WEAPONS—*Britain*

47, 48. *55in Boys Anti-Tank Rifle*

Originally of ·5in calibre, this weapon was designed by a Captain Boys and called the Stanchion gun, but renamed Boys on the designer's death. When it was first produced it met the British War Office specifications for a light anti-tank weapon to project a missile which would penetrate 14mm of armour at 20° at up to 500 yards range. In 1939 it was issued on a scale of one to each infantry platoon, but by that time its performance was already inadequate.

Basic data:

Weight: 36lb
Length overall: 64in
Barrel length: 30in
Feed: 5 round overhead box magazine
Sights: Aperture with two fixed settings—300 and 500 yards
Striking velocity at 100 yards: 2,840f/s which theoretically gave its bullet an ability to penetrate 16mm of armour at 500 yards
The "kick" of the Boys was considerable (71ft/lb as compared with 26ft/lb for a shotgun).

49. *P.I.A.T. Projector* ("Projector, Infantry, Anti-Tank") *Mk* 1

As a light weight replacement for the anti-tank rifle, the "P.I.A.T." served a useful interim purpose. Fired from the shoulder, it operated by means of ammunition fitted over a "spigot" or post containing a firing pin, and projected a bomb to about 100 yards. As well as armour piercing bombs it could, of course, also hurl smoke and anti-personnel bombs. As such, at one time it was suggested as a possible replacement for the 2in mortar.

Basic data:

   Weight: 32lb
   Length overall: 39in
   Bomb weight: 3lb
   Muzzle velocity: 450f/s
   Battle range: 100 yards (maximum range 750 yards)
   Sights: Pillar front, aperture rear with 70 and 100 yards setting.

50. *25mm Hotchkiss Anti-Tank Gun*

Large numbers of 25mm Hotchkiss guns were bought from the French at the beginning of the war, and one company of three platoons (each with three Hotchkiss guns) was organised in each first-line infantry brigade. Unfortunately the Hotchkiss was not sufficiently mobile for it to be deployed with the forward infantry and its armour penetration performance was soon found to be inadequate. Despite this the Hotchkiss was found to be a better weapon than its successor—the Boys rifle. But with the fall of France supplies of spares and ammunition were limited —a fact which speeded its replacement.

Basic data:

Weight of gun: 186lb
Weight of carriage: 1,083lb
Length of gun: 7ft 3in
Overall length of gun on carriage: 13ft 2in
Calibre: 25mm (·984in)

Action: Semi automatic
Penetration (Muzzle velocity 2,900f/s):
   42mm of armour at 20° at 500 yards
   40mm of armour at 35° at 200 yards

51-53. *Anti-Tank Guns*

The 2pr, 6pr and 17pr Anti-Tank guns which first supplemented and later replaced the British Boys anti-tank rifle, 25mm Hotchkiss and P.I.A.T. cannot properly be considered infantry equipments. As their designation implies they were "guns" in the true sense of the word—pieces of artillery which became more complex as the weight of shell increased. For this reason a description of their characteristics has been omitted.

51. *2pr Anti-Tank Gun*

52 (top). *6pr Anti-Tank Gun at Alamein, 1942*
53 (above). *17pr Anti-Tank Gun in Italy, 1945*

60

54

ANTI-TANK WEAPONS—*United States*

54–56. *2·36in "Bazooka"* (Rocket Launcher Anti-Tank, M1 and M9)

The rocket launcher A.T., M1 is a shoulder weapon consisting of a metal tube 54in long, 2·36in bore, open at both ends. It was generally fired by a 2-man team. The M9 differed from the M1 only in the barrel couplings.

Basic data:

Launcher:

Weight 13¼lb
Length overall: 5ft 1in
Maximum range: 700 yards
Sights: Fixed studs indicating 100, 200 and 300 yards

Ammunition (Rocket, H.E.A.T., 2·63in M6A3)

Weight: 3·4lb
Length: 21·62in
Diameter: 2·36in
Weight of H.E.: ·5lb

61

55 (top). *Projectile for Bazooka (M1)*

56 (above). *American Infantrymen Firing Bazooka*

57–58. *Recoilless Rifles.* 57mm M18 and 75mm M20

Basic data:

	57mm	75mm
Weight (gun complete):	40·25lb	103lb
Length overall:	46·44in	64·8in
Rifling:	Right hand, one turn in 30 calibres	Right hand, one turn in 22 calibres
Range (maximum):	4,400 yards	7,000 yards
Muzzle velocity:	1,200f/s	1,000f/s

59. *No. 36 Grenade.* Right, filled; Left, empty

GRENADES

	Britain	United States
Anti-Personnel:	36 1½lb; thrown by hand. 4 second fuse 70 1lb; used in Far East	Mk II and Mk 1A1 Similar to British 36
Anti-Tank:	Hawkins only 2¼lb; used as a mine to stop armoured vehicles by breaking tracks	H.E.A.T. rifle grenades projected from rifle
Smoke:	77⎫ 80⎭ About 1lb filled white phosphorus	M19 similar to British; can be projected from rifle

60. *Ack Pack Flame Thrower*

FLAME THROWERS

	Britain		United States
	(Ack Pack)*	(Wasp)	
Weight (in lbs)	49	1615	1475
Method of Carriage	Man Portable	Universal Carrier	Armoured Vehicle
Fuel capacity (in gallons)	4	79	79
Type of ignition	Cartridge— 10 two-second shots	Electric 2-second single shot	Electric Continuous or single shot
Maximum range in yards	50	120	180

* Illustrations 60 and 61 (overleaf).

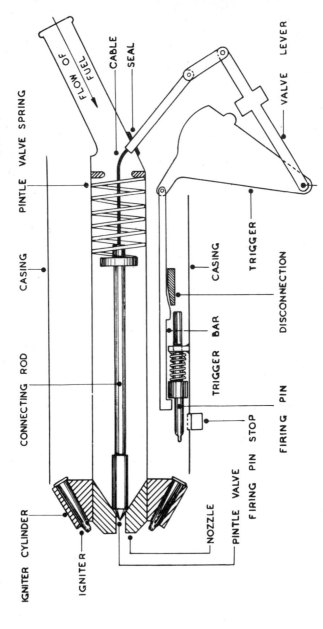

61. *British Ack Pack Flame Thrower*

FLOW OF FUEL

CABLE

SEAL

VALVE LEVER

PINTLE VALVE SPRING

CASING

PINTLE

CONNECTING ROD

CASING

TRIGGER

TRIGGER BAR

DISCONNECTION

FIRING PIN

FIRING PIN STOP

IGNITER CYLINDER

IGNITER

NOZZLE

PINTLE VALVE

66

APPENDIX 1

Comparative Weights for Equivalent Stopping Effect

Weapon	9mm Sten MC Mk 5	·45in Sub-MG M3	·45in Thompson Sub-MG	·45in Colt Pistol	9mm Browning Pistol
Weight of					
(a) Cartridge (grains)	183	322	322	322	183
(b) Magazine, empty (oz)	10·5	12·8	8·0	0·2	0·2
(c) Magazine, filled (lb)	1·5	2·3	1·9	0·5	0·6
Magazine capacity (rounds)	32	30	30	7	13
Mean figure of merit for damaging power over first 100 yards range	9·7	20·6	20·6	20·6	9·7
Number of bullets required for an equivalent damaging effect in more vulnerable parts	2·1	1	1	1	2·1
Number of rounds for equal stopping					
(a) 150 rounds ·45in	225	150	150	—	—
(b) 14 rounds ·45in	—	—	—	14	21
Number of					
(a) filled magazines required	7	5	5	2	2
(b) rounds in that of magazines	224	150	150	14	26
Weight of this load of filled magazines (lb)	10·4	11·4	9·4	1·0	1·2
Weight of weapons (lb)	8·4	8·1	10·8	2·4	2·1
Total weight (lb)	18·8	19·5	20·2	3·4	3·3

APPENDIX 2

This, and the table given in Appendix 1, has been compiled for the benefit of those concerned with the relative merits of British and U.S. pistols and sub-machine guns. Comparison of the "damaging" or "stopping" power of a weapon is a controversial subject. In military terms, what is meant is the ability to make a victim unable to fight even when the blow he receives is not in a vital spot. In close quarter fighting this is often a decisive factor—but so too can be the number of rounds and total weight carried by the man. However, for any given weight, a compromise between a few rounds with good "stopping power" and a large number of rounds of less stopping power is possible.

The "Figure of Merit" quoted is purely empirical—derived by the British Ordnance Board from the tentative formula $f\,d^2\,m\,v^{1.2}$, where

f = a design factor for the bullet (based on shape, material and stability)
d = bullet diameter in inches
m = weight of bullet in pounds
v = striking velocity in feet per second.

Estimated Damaging Power of Representative Pistol Cartridges

Bullet (type)	Weight (grains)	Velocity f/s yards from muzzle						Factor (e)	Dia. (ins)	Relative damaging power Figure of Merit		Length of barrel (ins)
		0	25	50	100	150	200			at PBR (g)	at 100 × (h)	
·38in (S & W)(a)	146	632	617	603	574	547	521	1·00*	0·359	6·1	5·5	5
9mm (Colt)(b)	130	1,190	1,139	1,096	1,026	971	924	0·90	0·359	10·6	8·8	5
·45in (M1911)(c)	234	920	894	871	831	798	767	0·90	0·450	21·9	19·4	5
·455in (Colt)(d)	255	738	687	651	586	526	473	1·05*	0·455	21·9	16·6	5·5

* Lead bullets.

NOTES
(a) This ·38in Smith & Wesson Revolver ammunition is possibly slightly less powerful than the British ·38in revolver cartridge as it has a less heavy bullet (146grs against 178grs).

(b) This ·38in Automatic Colt Pistol ammunition is somewhat more powerful than the British 9mm Parabellum cartridge as it has slightly heavier bullets (130gr against 115grs) and a somewhat higher muzzle velocity (1,190f/s against 1,110f/s when fired in a 5in barrel).

(c) This standard U.S. ·45 cartridge is somewhat less powerful than the British ·45in round as it has a slightly lower muzzle velocity (920f/s against 1,100f/s when fired in a 10·5in barrel).

(d) This ·45in Colt Revolver ammunition is somewhat more powerful than the British ·455in revolver cartridge as it has a slightly higher muzzle velocity (738f/s against 620f/s) though its bullet is somewhat lighter in weight (255grs against 265grs). Its lead bullet makes it somewhat more effective than the British enveloped bullet.

(e) These are the factors used to compensate for the presence or absence of a metal envelope and for the shape of the point in computing the damaging power of bullets in Textbooks of Pistols and Revolvers.

(g) Pistols are chiefly used at point blank range (PBR).

(h) Machine Carbines are seldom used in battle at ranges over 100 yards.

APPENDIX 3—Comparative Table of the Principal British, American and German Small Arms

Nationality	Weapon	Calibre	Weight	Approx. maximum range	Effective range	Cyclic rate of fire rpm
BRITISH	Pistol ·380 No 2	·375in	1lb 11½oz	Up to 30 yards	—	—
AMERICAN	Pistol Colt ·45 1911 Al Automatic	·45in	2lb 11oz	Up to 30 yards		—
GERMAN	Pistol "08" / Walther P 38	} 9mm (0·354in)	2lb / 2lb 5oz	} Up to 30 yards	—	—
BRITISH	SMLE Rifle No 1 / Rifle No 3 Mk 1 (Pattern 14)	·303in / ·303in	8lb 10½oz / 9lb ·6oz	2,000 yards / 2,000 yards	600 yards / 600 yards	— / —
AMERICAN	S/L Garand / S/L Carbine M 1	·300in / ·300in	9lb 7oz / 5lb 3oz	2,000 yards / 2,000 yards	600 yards / 300 yards	— / —
GERMAN	Rifle 98 / S/L Rifle G 41W / FG 42 Auto Rifle	} 7·92mm (·311in)	9lb / 10lb 14oz / 9lb 12oz	2,200 yards / 2,200 yards / 1,500 yards	600 yards / 600 yards / 300–600 yards	— / — / —
BRITISH	Sten Mk III	9mm	6·5lb	200 yards	30 yards	500–550
AMERICAN	M 3 SMG	·45in	6lb	200 yards	30 yards	450
GERMAN	Schmeisser MP 40 / MP 44	9mm / 7·92mm	9lb / 10lb	200 yards / 200 yards	30 yards / 30 yards	450–540 / 800

BRITISH	Bren Vickers	} .303in	23lb 30lb *without* tripod	2,000 yards 3,500–4,000 yards	800 yards 800–1,200 yards	450–550 500
AMERICAN	Browning Auto Rifle M 1918 Johnson LMG (used by the U.S. Marines) Browning MMG	} .300	17lb 15lb 33lb	2,000 yards 2,000 yards 3,500–4,000 yards	600 yards 600 yards 800–1,200 yards	500 450–750 400–520
GERMAN	MG 34 MG 42	} 7·92mm	26lb 24lb	2,750 yards 2,750 yards	800 yards 800 yards	800–900 1,200

APPENDIX 4

Comparative Table of British, American and German Infantry Mortars

Nationality	Designation	Calibre inches	Total WT lbs	Remarks
1. LIGHT MORTARS				
British	2in Mk 2* Mk 2** Mk 7	2	21	2in mortar with a large baseplate
	2in Mk 2*** Mk 7** Mk 8	2	11	2in mortar with full-length barrel and spade base-plate
	2in Mk 7*	2	9	Airborne 2in mortar with shortened barrel and spade base plate
American	60mm M 2	2·3	42	A muzzle loading smooth bore weapon of conventional Stokes–Brandt design. This was a platoon weapon in the American Army
	60mm Mortar T 18E6	2·3	19½	This weapon consisted of a 60mm M2 barrel fired from a spade baseplate—making it not unlike the latest British 2in mortar. Only a limited number was manufactured
German	5cm GrW 36	2	31	Muzzle loaded, smooth bore mortar. Broke down into two loads; the baseplate, traversing and cross-levelling gear: the barrel and elevating gear. Mortars made after 1938 had no sights. Mortar would only fire high angle
2. MEDIUM MORTARS				
British	3in Mk 5	3·2	112	The lightest British 3in mortar. Conventional Stokes–Brandt design
American	81mm M 1	3·2	141	A muzzle loading smooth bore weapon of conventional Stokes–Brandt design. This weapon was an exact copy of the Italian 81mm mortar and corresponded to the 3in British mortar
American	81mm T 27 (Short 81mm)	3·2	66	A cut down version of the 81mm M1 using a 60mm mortar baseplate. Only a limited number was made
German	8cm short GrW 42	3·2	62	A cut down version of the 8cm long GW 34 Weight compared with the 8cm long GW 34 as follows: Short Long Barrel 22¼ 40 Bipod 21½ 40 Baseplate 10½ 44
German	8cm long GrW 34	3·2	125	A muzzle loaded, smooth bore mortar of conventional Stokes-Brandt design

Bombs Type	WT lbs	No. of charges	Max range yards	Remarks
HE	2¼	1	500	
Smoke bursting	2¼	1	500	
Smoke emission	2	1	500	
Illuminating	1	1	—	Reached a height of 500ft at 85 degrees
Multi-star				(Max. range of the airborne mortar was 350 yards)
White	2	1	—	
Red	1	1	—	
Green	1	1	—	
Red and Green	1	1	—	
Smoke bursting	—	—	—	
HE	3	5	1,984	Max. practical range of the T 18E6 was 350 yards
Illuminating	—	5	1,000	
HE	2	1	570	This range was considered inadequate in North Africa and the weapon was soon regarded as obsolete
HE	10	2	2,790	
Smoke bursting	10	2	2,790	
Base ejection smoke	—	2	2,790	Fitted with a time fuse, it was also used for coloured smoke and flares (Only 5,000 were made)
Star	10	1	—	
Smoke emission	10	2	2,790	
HE	7	6	3,280	
HE	10¾	4	2,655	
HE	15	4	1,280	
Smoke bursting	11½	4	2,470	
Illuminating	11½	4	2,766	
HE	7	–	1,935	
HE	10¾	–	1,360	The ammunition was the same as for the 81mm M1, but the range was naturally less
HE	15	–	—	
Smoke bursting	11½	–	—	
Illuminating	11½	–	—	
HE	7¾	3	1,200	
Bursting smoke	7¾	3	1,200	
Indicating	7¾	3	1,200	Emitted blue smoke
Incendiary	—	–	—	
Illuminating			—	
Jumping bomb	7¾	3	1,200	

All bombs were the same as for the long mortar but used a maximum of two secondaries instead of four

HE	7¾	5	2,625	
Bursting smoke	7¾	5	2,625	
Indicating	7¾	5	2,625	Emitted blue smoke
Incendiary	—	–	—	
Illuminating			—	
Jumping	7¾	5	2,625	

APPENDIX 5

Small Arms Ammunition Interchangeability

Even if allied nations do not standardise their weapons, the convenience of ammunition common to all is obvious. Production is simplified and supply in the field is made easier. In war it is often also desirable to be able to use one's own ammunition in captured weapons—even if some risk is involved, as is likely when the chamber of the weapon does not match the alien cartridges. Many weapons have been reported as being capable of firing standard British or United States ammunition and the following table summarizes the available information. It must, however, be stressed that in many cases no firing trials have been conducted to prove the veracity of this information, and it must be assumed that any attempt to fire ammunition other than that specifically prescribed for the relevant weapon may be extremely hazardous.

Weapons are listed with the relevant British and U.S. ammunition.

Pistols

6·35mm Finnish Pistol	U.S. ·25in ACP Ball
7·63mm German 1894 Mauser	U.S. 7·63mm Mauser

7·65mm Belgian Brownings
7·65mm Danish Ruby
7·65mm French Ruby
7·65mm French Star
7·65mm German Walther (PP and PPK)
7·65mm German Mauser
7·65mm German Behalln — British SAA ·32in Mk 1z
7·65mm German Dreyse — U.S. Ball ·32in Colt auto
7·65mm German Sauer
7·65mm Italian Beretta
7·65mm Spanish M 19
7·65mm Swedish Ahlberg

9mm Belgian Brownings (Colt action)
9mm Czech VZ 22, VZ 24, VZ 39
9mm Finnish Lahti
9mm German M/08 Luger
9mm German Mauser 1898 — British SAA 9mm Mk 1z
9mm German P38 Walther — U.S. 9mm M 1 Parabellum
9mm Italian Beretta
9mm Polish M 35
9mm Swedish M 40 Lahti

Rifles

7·92mm German Gewehr 98
7·92mm German KAR 98 K
    Mauser
7·92mm German Gewehr 41 M

⎫
⎮
⎬
⎮
⎭

British SAA 7·92mm Ball Mk 2
British SAA 7·92mm Tracer
  G Mk 2
British SAA 7·92mm SA
  AP Mk 3
U.S. 7·92mm Ball M 1

Sub-Machine Guns

7·63mm German Mauser ..   .. U.S. 7·63mm Mauser

9mm Austrian M/34 Steyr–Solothurn
9mm Danish M/46 (P-16) Madsen
9mm Finnish Model 31 Suomi
9mm German MP 18
9mm German MP 38
9mm German MP 40
9mm Italian M/38 Beretta
9mm Italian Villa Peroxa
9mm Swedish M 37/39 Suomi

⎫
⎮
⎮
⎮
⎬
⎮
⎮
⎮
⎭

British SAA 9mm Mk 1z
U.S. 9mm M 1 auto

Machine Guns

7·7mm Italian Breda–Safat

⎧
⎨
⎩

British SAA ·303in Mk 82
British SAA ·303in AP Mk 1
British SAA ·303in Observing Mk 1

7·92mm Japanese Type 98
7·92mm Japanese Type 100
7·92mm Japanese Type 01

7·92mm German MG 15
7·92mm German MG 34
7·92mm German MG 42

⎫
⎮
⎮
⎬
⎮
⎮
⎭

British SAA 7·92mm Ball Mk 2
British SAA 7·92mm Tracer G
  Mk 2
British SAA 7·92mm SA AP Mk 2
U.S. 7·92mm Ball M 1

75

APPENDIX 6

Note on the Comparative Effectiveness of British and German Mortars

During the campaign in North Africa British troops complained bitterly that enemy mortars were causing many more casualties than their own weapons. A series of trials were arranged to verify this and to compare the accuracy of the British 3in and German 81mm mortars. The results showed that although the German weapons were no more accurate and their bombs no more lethal than their British counterparts the British mortar was outranged by both the Italian and German mortars.

Ranges for mortars used in North Africa were:

Italian 7lb bomb	..	.. 4,400 yards
Italian 15lb bomb	..	.. 1,600 yards
German 7lb bomb	..	.. 2,600 yards
British 10lb bomb	..	.. 1,600 yards

To rectify this the British bomb was fitted with extra secondary charges (necessitating the base plate of the mortar's being strengthened). This gave the 10lb bomb a range of 2,600 yards—equivalent to that of the German 81mm.

In effect, the British suffered more casualties from mortars because the Germans handled their weapons differently. In many cases German mortars were fired in batteries, whereas this was rarely the British practice. They also used their mortars repeatedly, and with deadly effect, on positions from which they had just withdrawn and where the British troops were digging in—such bombardments often being the prelude to a counter-attack.